Mini Lop R

The moral rights of the author has been asserted
British Library Cataloguing in Publication Data
A catalogue record for this book is available from the British Library

ISBN 978-1-909820-10-4

Disclaimer and Legal Notice

Mini Lop Rabbits

The Complete Owner's Guide
to Mini Lop Bunnies

How to Care for your Mini Lop Eared Rabbit,
Including Breeding, Lifespan, Colors, Health,
Personality, Diet and Facts

Ann L. Fletcher

Foreword

Hello and thank you for buying my book.

In this book you will find some wonderful information to help you care for your Mini Lop Rabbits. I've included in this book information about Mini Lop Rabbit care, habitat, cages, enclosures, diet, facts, set up, food, pictures, life span, breeding, feeding cost and a care sheet. After reading this book you will be a lot more confident in looking after your Mini Lop Rabbit!

I have written this book using American spelling as that is what I'm used to. I have given measurements in both feet and inches/pounds and ounces and also in metric. I have also given costs in US$ and GBP. Both the measurements and costs are approximate guides. I have done my best to ensure the accuracy of the information in this book as at the time of publishing.

I trust that after reading this book you will feel more confident about owning and looking after a Mini Lop Rabbit and that you have a wonderful time enjoying the pleasure they bring in the years to come!

All good wishes, Ann L. Fletcher

Acknowledgements

I would like to extend my sincerest thanks to my dear friend Jane for all her input in assisting me put this book together. She has long experience of looking after Mini Lops and without her feedback I'm sure I'd have missed something.

Additional thanks to my husband John and our children Mark and Stacey for their love and patience as Mom taps away on her computer. Their understanding and love for my passion made the whole journey worthwhile.

Table of Contents

Chapter One: Introduction

M ini Lop Rabbits are one of several medium-sized rabbit breeds with pendulous ears. These rabbits resemble a dwarfed lop rabbit, having lopped ears and small, compact bodies with an average weight when fully grown of around 5 lbs. (2.27 kg). Mini Lops comes in a wide range of colors and patterns so you can find one to suit your individual preferences. Best of all, these rabbits are incredibly gentle and friendly as pets!

The Mini Lop Rabbit is known for its diminutive size, its lopped ears and its friendly nature. These rabbits make excellent family pets because they are very comfortable around people as well as other household pets. As long as your rabbit is properly socialized and your other pets well-behaved, you should have no trouble keeping a Mini Lop with other pets in the house.

This breed of rabbit has been around since the early 1970s, but it has begun to grow in popularity in recent years. These rabbits are not only cute and cuddly – they are also very intelligent! Mini Lops can be litter trained and they can also be taught to obey simple commands and to perform basic tricks. If you are looking for a smart and loveable pet for yourself or your family, the Mini Lop Rabbit is definitely a good choice to consider!

Useful Terms to Know:

- **Buck**: a male rabbit

- **Cross Breeding**: breeding two different breeds together

- **Crown**: refers to a prominent ridge and crest along the top of the head extending to the base of the ears

- **Dam**: the mother of a rabbit

- **Doe**: a female rabbit

- **Hock**: the joint of the rabbit's foot

- **Inbreeding**: breeding two closely related rabbits to each other (e.g. brother to sister)

- **Junior**: young rabbit between 14 weeks and 5 months

- **Kindling**: process of giving birth to a litter of kits

- **Kit**: a baby rabbit

- **Litter**: two or more baby rabbits resulting from a single pregnancy/kindling

- **Lopped**: pendulous ears (opposite of erect ears)

- **Stud Buck**: a male rabbit suitable for breeding

- **Sire**: the father of a rabbit

- **Weaning**: the process through which kits begin to eat more solid food and rely less on nursing

Chapter Two: Understanding Mini Lops

1) What Are Mini Lop Rabbits?

The Mini Lop Rabbit is a breed of domestic rabbit that has become very popular throughout the United States of America. This breed is the third smallest of all the lop rabbit breeds and it is the smallest non-dwarfed lop.

Despite not actually being a dwarfed breed, the Mini Lop in the U.K. is commonly known as the Dwarf Lop. In the U.K.

there is a breed of domestic rabbit known as the Miniature Lop but it is the equivalent of the Holland Lop in the U.S.A.

Mini Lop Rabbits are exactly what their name implies – they are small rabbits with lopped ears. This breed was developed in Germany during the second half of the twentieth century and it was first debuted in the U.S. in 1974. This breed is popular for its attractive appearance as well as its friendly and playful personality. Mini Lops are also very intelligent as they can be trained to follow simple commands and to perform tricks.

If you are looking for a friendly family pet, the Mini Lop Rabbit is definitely a good option. These rabbits remain small so they do not require as much space as other popular rabbit breeds. Though their size may be diminutive compared to that of other breeds, but they have just as much love to give. Mini Lop Rabbits can bond closely with their families and they will not thrive if neglected. If you have the time to dedicate to properly caring for a rabbit, the Mini Lop is certainly an excellent choice.

2) Facts about Mini Lop Rabbits

Mini Lop Rabbits are classified as medium-sized and they have been nicknamed the "basketball with a head" due to their body shape. These rabbits are known for their round, thick set bodies with long ears, a wide head and thick bone structure. The "type" of this breed is described in the breed standard as "short with well-rounded loins, deep chest and wide shoulders… cobby well-muscled appearance."

The ears of this breed are incredibly important when it comes to the breed standard. A Mini Lops ears should sit close against the cheeks with the ear openings turned in. They should hang between ¾ and 1 inch (1.91 and 2.54 cm.) below the jaw and be rounded on the ends and well-furred. Folds in the ear that are extremely thick or thin are considered to be a fault. This is only a concern if you are intending to 'show' your rabbit but if you are just looking for a pet to join your family, it is absolutely nothing to worry about!

Mini Lop Rabbits come in a wide range of colors. Their fur is typically thick and dense with a glossy, lustrous appearance. Most Mini Lops have coats that are medium in length – very short fur is considered a fault. These rabbits can exhibit a wide range of colors and patterns, either solid or broken. The eyes can be any color, but it is a fault if the eyes do not match each other.

Summary of Mini Lop Rabbits Facts

Classification: small breed

Alternative Names: dwarf lop (UK)

Weight: the maximum weight defined by the ARBA weight limits and showroom classes is 6.5 lbs. (2.72 kg) in U.S.A. and as defined by the BRC in the UK is 5 lbs. 4 oz. (2.38 kg)

Body Shape: medium-sized, thick set and round

Body Structure: heavily muscled, well balanced

Coat: medium-length, thick and dense

Coat Color: black, blue, blue-eyed white, chestnut agouti, chinchilla, chocolate, orange, opal, lynx, lilac, tri color, ruby-eyed white and white

Lifespan: average 7 to 10 years

3) History of Mini Lop Rabbits as Pets

Bob Herschbach is credited with the discovery of the Mini Lop breed in 1972. Herschbach first saw the Mini Lop at a German National Rabbit Show in Essen, Germany – at the time, the breed was known as the Klein Widder. These rabbits were the result of a cross between the German Big Lop and a smaller breed known as the Chinchilla. Originally, these two breeds came only in white and agouti colors so these are the colors early Mini Lops exhibited as well.

Once he returned home to the United States, Herschbach began breeding Mini Lops himself. The first generation of kits exhibited solid colors but the second generation had broken color. In 1974, Herschbach brought his Mini Lops to an American Rabbit Breeders Association (ARBA) convention in Ventura, California. In addition to changing the name from Klein Widder to Mini Lop, the ARBA also suggested that he downsize the breed to achieve a more compact and attractive rabbit.

In 1977, sponsorship of the Mini Lop breed passed to Herb Dyke. The following year, Dyke and Herschbach started a correspondence club for the Mini Lop breed. In less than a year the club had grown to more than 500 members. In 1980, the Mini Lop appeared at the National Rabbit Convention in Milwaukee, Wisconsin and was awarded the title of an official breed sanctioned by the ARBA. Shortly after its acceptance by the ARBA, Dyke and Herschbach's correspondence club was transformed into the first national breed club – the Mini Lop Club of America.

a) History of the American Rabbit Breeders Association

The American Rabbit Breeders Association (ARBA) was founded in 1910 and has its headquarters in Bloomington, Illinois. The purpose of this association is to promote rabbit fancy and to facilitate commercial rabbit production. The ARBA is responsible for setting breed standards and sanctioning rabbit shows throughout North America.

In addition to sponsoring local clubs and fairs, the ARBA holds a national convention show annually, drawing rabbit fanciers from around the globe.

Not only does the ARBA set breed standards and organize shows, it also serves to provide rabbit raising education.

Every five years the ARBA publishes a detailed guide for rabbit fanciers called *Standard of Perfection*. The ARBA also publishes educational materials like guidebooks and posters including photographs of all the recognized rabbit breeds. Additionally, the ARBA has a library of over 10,000 books and writings on domestic rabbits which is the largest single repository of its kind.

b) History of the British Rabbit Council

The breeding and showing of rabbits began over two hundred years ago. Throughout the nineteenth century, fanciers gathered to form local clubs for showing and improving individual breeds. The number of rabbit breeds recognized increased throughout the 1800s and early 1900s but by 1918, the most popular breed by far was the Beveren. In May of 1918 breeders of Beveren rabbits gathered to form a national club called The Beveren Club.

The Beveren Club served to raise the profile of rabbit breeding, adopting and standardizing new breeds. Eventually, the name of the club changed to the British Fur Rabbit Society and then to the British Rabbit Society. By 1928, over a dozen different breeds were recognized and interest in rabbit breeding began to grow. As a result, a new club was formed called the National Rabbit Council of Great Britain. The club grew quickly but conflicts arose between the two clubs which led to them eventually merging in 1934 to form the British Rabbit Council.

4) *Mini Lop Rabbit Colors*

The color groups exhibited by the Mini Lop Breed include: self, agouti, shaded, broken, ticked and wide band. These color groups are separated into two classifications by the ARBA: solid pattern and broken pattern. Mini Lops may also exhibit colors that are not currently recognized by the ARBA including: otter, harlequin, silver marten, blue seal and blue point. If however, your main concern is having a Mini Lop as a pet, then you only have to worry about your personal preference and not worry about 'show' standards.

Self

The word "self" is used in regard to rabbits that exhibit a single color all over the body including its ears, head, feet and tail. Self-colored Mini Lop Rabbits can be seen in black, white, chocolate and blue.

Agouti

An agouti pattern is one in which the top and side of the rabbit's body are banded and ticked with color. Ticked simply means that the tips of the hairs are a different color.

There are several color variations for the agouti pattern including: chestnut, chinchilla and opal.

Shaded

Shaded Mini Lops exhibit darker coloring on the legs, feet, ears, tail and head with the color fading to a lighter shade on the body. Some of the color patterns seen in this category include: Siamese sable, Siamese smoke, seal point and sooty fawn.

Broken

A broken pattern is simply any color combined with white – the body color should be broken evenly and there should be color on the nose, around each eye and on the ears. Ideally, broken lops should have between 10% and 70% color. It is preferred that the rabbit exhibit a butterfly marking on the nose outlined in white with colored ears and eye circles. The front feet should be white and the back feet may be colored, but it is not required.

Ticked

Mini Lop Rabbits are said to be "ticked" when the tips of the hairs are a different color. These rabbits possess the steel gene and may exhibit ticking in either gold or silver. Colors for ticked rabbits may include black, blue, chocolate, lilac, silver fox, sable or smoke pearl.

Wide Band

Mini Lop Rabbits in the wide band category look very similar to those with the agouti pattern. Instead of the secondary color showing around the eyes, tail and ears, it shows in a layer – the rabbit will exhibit one color on top and a second on the bottom half of the body. Some of the colors seen in this category include: cream, fawn, orange, red and frosty.

Chapter Three: What to Know Before You Buy

1) Do You Need a License?

Now that you've learned the basics about this wonderful breed you can move on to thinking about what you need to do before you buy your Mini Lop Rabbits. Before you even start to think about where you are going to get your rabbit you need to determine whether you are required to have a license or permit to keep Mini Lop Rabbits in your area.

a) Licensing in the U.S.

There is no federal law in the United States requiring private rabbit owners to obtain a license for keeping Mini Lop Rabbits. There are, however, certain state laws regarding the keeping and breeding of domestic rabbits. The state of Minnesota, for example, requires rabbit owners to pay a $15 annual fee to license their pet rabbit – a higher fee may be charged if the rabbit is not spayed or neutered.

Generally, retail pet store owners and private collectors are not required to obtain a permit for keeping Mini Lop Rabbits. If you plan to breed your rabbits for wholesale or exhibition, however, you may need to obtain a license. To determine the requirements for your particular area, check with your local council. It is better to be safe than sorry – especially if failing to license your rabbit could cost you hefty fines.

b) Licensing in the U.K.

The U.K. does not have any legislation requiring rabbit owners or breeders to obtain a license. There are, however, laws in place in regard to importing or exporting animals. Rabies has long been eradicated from the U.K. and strict import and export laws are now in place to prevent the disease from being re-introduced. If you plan to bring a rabbit with you to the U.K., or if you plan to export one, you will need to obtain an animal movement license (AML).

c) Licensing Outside the U.S and U.K.

Licensing requirements for Mini Lop Rabbits vary from one country or region to another. One of the only cases in which the ownership of pet rabbits is expressly prohibited is in Queensland, Australia. Rabbits are not a native species in Queensland – they are actually considered a Class 2 pest by the Land Protection Act of 2002. A penalty of Australian $44,000 can be levied as a result flaunting this law.

As they are not a native species, rabbits can threaten the survival of certain native species and also cause damage to the environment. You cannot obtain a license to keep a pet rabbit in Queensland because it is illegal. The only time in which a permit may be issued is if the rabbit is being used for research or entertainment purposes.

2) How Many Should You Buy?

Mini Lop Rabbits are very social creatures by nature. This being the case, many inexperienced rabbit owners assume that it is best to keep them with others of their own kind. The fact that Mini Lops are very social does not necessarily mean they need to be kept in pairs or in groups – it simply means that your rabbit requires a significant amount of daily interaction in order to thrive.

Keeping more than one rabbit in the same living space can be tricky. While Mini Lops are friendly and gentle creatures by nature, you can never know for sure how a rabbit will react to another rabbit entering its territory. In the wild, rabbit colonies tend to form a strict hierarchy and they have been known to defend their territory.

If you try to keep two rabbits together and one is more dominant than the other, the subservient rabbit could become stressed and fall ill due to the bullying of the other rabbit.

If you truly want to form a close bond with your rabbit, it is best to keep only one. Your rabbit doesn't need another rabbit companion as long as you give it plenty of love and attention yourself. In fact, your rabbit is more likely to bond with you if you do not keep it with another rabbit.

If, however, you do want to keep more than one rabbit together it is best to buy them when they are the same age so they can be raised together. It is not a good idea to add a new rabbit to an already established cage – this is likely to cause territorial issues.

3) Can Mini Lop Rabbits Be Kept with Other Pets?

Like most rabbit breeds, Mini Lop Rabbits are very gentle and playful by nature. This being the case, these rabbits can generally be kept with other pets. If you plan to keep your rabbit with other household pets it is important that you socialize your rabbit properly and supervise the time your rabbit spends with other pets. While your other pets may not be aggressive by nature, animal behavior is difficult to predict and it is always better to be safe than sorry.

My best advice is not to take any chances but ultimately you must make a judgment call as you are best placed to know the character of your pets.

Follow these tips when keeping a Mini Lop Rabbit in the same house as other pets:

- Make sure your rabbit has a safe place to retreat to if he wants to

- Always supervise your Mini Lops time with other pets to prevent accidents

- Do not keep Mini Lops with ferrets – ferrets are predatory animals and may injure your rabbit

- Mini Lops can bond with a variety of pets including cats, dogs and guinea pigs

- Prevent your rabbit from accessing the food of other pets (cats, dogs etc.)

- Rabbits may not get along with birds – due to their sensitive ears, noisy birds may irritate rabbits

- Mini Lops can be kept in the same house as pets that are housed in tanks such as fish and frogs, as long as you prevent them from chewing on electrical cords

4) Ease and Cost of Care

Mini Lop Rabbits are an excellent choice for a family pet because they are gentle, friendly and love to have the attention of their human companions. Before you go out and buy a rabbit, however, you should be sure that you can handle the initial and on-going monthly costs.

The initial costs of a Mini Lop Rabbit include the purchase price of the rabbit itself plus the cost of spay/neuter surgery, microchipping and initial vaccinations as well as the cost of the cage and accessories. Once you cover these costs you must also think about monthly costs such as food, bedding and veterinary care.

Think about all of these overheads before you decide to buy a Mini Lop Rabbit.

a) Initial Costs

Initial costs for keeping a Mini Lop Rabbit are those required to buy your rabbit and to prepare its cage. In addition to the cage and the rabbit itself you will need to pay for de-sexing (assuming you are not planning to breed your rabbit) and microchipping the rabbit as well as any initial vaccinations the rabbit needs. Add to these the cost of preparing the rabbit's cage and stocking up on accessories and you will find the initial cost of keeping a Mini Lop Rabbit.

Purchase Price: The price of a Mini Lop Rabbit will vary depending where you buy it. You may be able to find these rabbits at your local pet store for around $20 to $25 (£13 - £16.25). These rabbits are not guaranteed to be pedigreed, however. Pedigreed Mini Lop Rabbits bred for show tend to be more expensive than other rabbits – they can cost as much as $40 to $60 (£26 to £39).

Spay/Neuter: If you do not plan to breed your rabbits, it is normally a good idea to spay or neuter them. The cost of the spay/neuter surgery is generally around $100 (£65) but you may be able to find a lower price at a veterinary clinic in your area. Seek advice from your vet on the pros and cons of having your rabbit spayed or neutered.

Microchipping: A microchip is a tiny electronic device that is inserted under your rabbit's skin. This device is used to store your contact information so if the rabbit is lost, you can be contacted. It is not a requirement that you have your rabbit microchipped, but it is certainly a good idea. The cost of this procedure is generally about $30 (£19.50).

Vaccinations: One of the first things you need to do when you get a new rabbit is to have it examined by a veterinarian and caught up on its vaccinations. Costs for veterinary care may vary depending where you live but the average cost for initial vaccinations is around $50 (£32.50).

Cage: Mini Lop Rabbits are a very small breed, weighing on average 5 lbs. (2.27 kg) at maturity. This being the case, they do not require a cage as large as some breeds. It is important, however, that you provide your rabbits with plenty of space to hop around and stretch out.

You may also choose to let your rabbit roam free throughout the house. Even if you do that, you should have a cage or hutch where your rabbit can sleep at night. The cost for a rabbit's cage will vary depending on size and materials, but you should be ready to spend around $200 to $300 (£130 to £195).

Accessories: To prepare your rabbit's cage you will need to stock up on a few accessories. These accessories might include a water bottle, food bowl, bedding and chew toys for your rabbit. Another accessory that would be good to have around is a travel carrier – this will be useful when you need to take your rabbit to the vet. The cost of initial accessories may be around $100 (£65).

Additional Costs: In addition to purchasing your rabbit as well as his cage and accessories, there are a few additional costs you should be prepared for. Some of these costs might include a litter pan, grooming supplies and cleaning equipment. For the most part, these tools and supplies should last you for several years and the total cost may average around $100 (£65).

Summary of Initial Costs

Cost Type	One Rabbit	Two Rabbits
Purchase Price	$20 - $60 (£13 - £39)	$40 to $120 (£26 - £78)
Spay/Neuter	$100 (£65)	$200 (£130)
Microchipping	$30 (£19.50)	$60 (£39)
Vaccinations	$50 (£32.50)	$100 (£65)
Cage or Pen	$200 to $300 (£130 - £195)	$200 to $300 (£130 - £195)
Cage Accessories	$100 (£65)	$100 (£65)
Other Tools/Equipment	$100 (£65)	$100 (£65)
Total:	$600 - $740 (£390 - £481)	$800 - $980 (£520 - £637)

b) Monthly Costs

In addition to these initial costs you should also be ready to pay for several other costs on a monthly basis. In order to properly care for your Mini Lop Rabbit you will need to buy fresh food and bedding every month – you may also need to provide routine veterinary care. Additionally, you should be prepared to pay for additional costs such as replacing accessories or making repairs to the cage. Below you will find an explanation of the monthly costs you can come to expect as a Mini Lop Rabbit owner.

Food: Your monthly costs for rabbit food will vary depending how many rabbits you keep and what type of food you buy. Some of the types of food you will need to buy for your rabbits include greens, hay, commercial rabbit pellets and fresh vegetables. The cost to feed a single Mini Lop Rabbit for one month averages about $30 (£19.50).

Bedding: If you plan to keep your rabbit in its cage or hutch, your bedding costs may be higher than if you let your rabbit roam free throughout the house. Your monthly cost for bedding will also depend on the type of bedding you buy. In general, you should plan to spend up to $50 (£32.50) per month on bedding. You can reduce your bedding costs by using recycled newspapers but do not use colored magazines because the ink may contain toxins that are harmful to your rabbit.

Veterinary Care: If you care for your Mini Lop properly, you should not have to worry about veterinary care on a monthly basis. You should, however, take your rabbit to the vet for a check-up once a year. The total yearly cost for this is generally around $50 (£32.50) which is less than $5 (£3.25) per month. However, you cannot predict veterinary expenses if your rabbit becomes unexpectedly ill and should have savings for this or could consider pet insurance. Please see Chapter 6 for more details.

Additional Costs: Other monthly costs you should be prepared for include replacing chew toys and making repairs to the cage or supplies. These costs are generally not very high and may only be $24 (£15.60) per year which is $2 (£1.30) per month.

Summary of Monthly Costs

Cost Type	One Rabbit	Two Rabbits
Food	$30 (£19.50)	$60 (£39)
Bedding	$50 (£32.50)	$50 (£32.50)
Veterinary Care	$5 (£3.25)	$10 (£6.50)
Additional Costs	$2 (£1.30)	$4 (£2.60)
Total:	$87 (£56.55)	$124 (£80.60)

c) Time Considerations

In addition to the initial and monthly costs for keeping Mini Lop rabbits, you also need to think about the amount of care these animals require and the time that this will take. Though Mini Lop Rabbits are not difficult to keep as pets, they do require regular maintenance. Refer to the following lists to get an idea how much time you will need to dedicate to your rabbit's care on a daily and weekly basis:

Daily Tasks to Complete:

- Clean food dish and refresh food

- Clean water bottle and refresh water

- Moving rabbit to exercise pen (20 to 30 minutes daily)

- Interacting with the rabbit

- Observation/basic health check

Estimated Daily Commitment*: 1 hour*

Weekly Tasks to Complete:

- Completely replacing bedding

- Cleaning out cage and accessories

- More detailed health check

- Spending extended time interacting with rabbit

- Checking ears, nails and teeth

- Combing/brushing rabbit (when molting you may need to do this daily)

Estimated Weekly Commitment: 10 hours

5) Human Health Considerations

Before you buy you also need to consider any implications to your own health. For example, do you know if you have an allergy or sensitivity to rabbits? I would recommend taking advice from your Doctor to ensure that you understand the implications to your own health and if necessary, are allergy tested.

6) Pros and Cons of Mini Lop Rabbits

Choosing the right breed of rabbit for you and your family can be difficult. To help you make your decision, consult this list of pros and cons for Mini Lop Rabbits:

Pros for Mini Lop Rabbits

- Small size means they require less space than other rabbit breeds and larger pets

- Very friendly and playful breed by nature

- Intelligent – can be trained to perform tricks and respond to simple commands

- Fairly easy to litter train – makes clean-up easier

- Can bond closely with human companions

- Docile personality – can get along with cats, dogs and other household pets

Cons for Mini Lop Rabbits

- Not a good choice for very busy owners – require a lot of human attention and interaction

- Needs a lot of chew toys to keep teeth filed down

- Requires a specific diet in order to remain healthy

- Needs just as much care as a dog or cat – not especially difficult but not the kind of pet you can just forget about

- Can become destructive if allowed to roam freely – will chew on cords and furniture

- Cage will take up space in the home if kept indoors – odor can also be unpleasant

Chapter Four: Purchasing Mini Lop Rabbits

1) Where to Buy Mini Lop Rabbits

Once you've decided that a Mini Lop Rabbit is definitely the right choice for you, your next step is to find your rabbit! When it comes to buying Mini Lop Rabbits, you have several options to choose from. As this breed is not one of the most common rabbit breeds you may not be able to find them in your local pet store as they might only carry a few selected breeds. If you plan to breed your rabbits or train them for show, you should plan to purchase from an independent breeder anyway. For those who simply want a Mini Lop Rabbit as a pet, another excellent option is to adopt a rabbit from your local rabbit rescue group.

a) Buying in the U.S.

In the United States, you may be able to find Mini Lop Rabbits at your local pet store depending on how large a selection they have. Keep in mind, however, that rabbits sold at pet stores may not be bred from high-quality stock and they may be more likely to be exposed to disease. Even if you do not buy from the pet store, you may still be able to get information about local breeders in your area. You might also try asking your veterinarian for a referral.

Another option is to perform an online search for Mini Lop Rabbit breeders. You can often find listings of breeders on national websites such as the American Rabbit Breeders Association. If all else fails, look for a rabbit rescue in your area. You may not find a rescue that has baby rabbits available, but adult rabbits are likely to already be litter trained and are more likely to be up to date on their vaccinations.

U.S.A. Breeder Websites:

"National Breeders Listing," Mini Lop Rabbit Club of America, http://minilop.org/bdirectory.html

State Rabbit Breeders Index, http://rabbitbreeders.us/state-rabbit-breeders-index

You may also be able to find Mini Lop Rabbits at a rabbit rescue in your area. Try these websites to adopt a rabbit:

National Rabbit Rescue Group Directory, http://rabbit.rescueshelter.com/USA

"Resources for Animal Shelters," House Rabbit Society, http://rabbit.org/resources-for-animal-shelters/

b) Buying in the U.K.

Despite the selection of breeds kept, it is highly unlikely that you will be able to find Mini/ Dwarf Lop Rabbits at your local pet store in the U.K. though. As is true in the U.S., you should be aware that rabbits sold at pet stores may not be bred from high-quality stock. If you can't locate any to buy from a pet store, ask your veterinarian or fellow rabbit owners for a referral to a breeder. Another option is to check the breeder listings on the British Rabbit Council or National French and Dwarf Lop Club websites.

U.K. Breeder Websites:

National French and Dwarf Lop Club
http://www.nfdlc.com

"Lop Rabbit Breeders," RabbitBreeders.org.uk,
http://rabbitbreeders.org.uk/lop-rabbit-breeders

Scottish Dwarf Lops and Mini Lops
http://www.scottishdwarflops.co.uk

You may also be able to find Mini/Dwarf Lop Rabbits at a rabbit rescue in your area. Try these websites to adopt a rabbit:

UK Rabbit Rescue Group Directory,
http://rabbit.rescueshelter.com/uk

Pre-Loved, Mini/Dwarf Lops Available for Adoption,
www.preloved.co.uk/adverts/list/3659/rabbits.html?keywor
·d=dwarf%20lop

Rabbit Rehome UK: www.rabbitrehome.org.uk

The Rabbit Residence Rescue: www.rabbitresidence.org.uk

**Note: Purchasing animals online is dangerous and can be considered cruel because it is difficult to regulate the treatment of animals during shipping – they may be exposed to extreme temperatures and/or rough handling.

Please avoid buying Mini Lop Rabbits online. In fact, if this is your only option, then please reconsider having a pet at all. It just isn't worth it!

2) How to Select a Healthy Mini Lop Rabbit

Owning and caring for a Mini Lop Rabbit is more than just a responsibility – it is a privilege. These creatures are an absolute joy to have around and as the owner; it is your duty to keep your rabbit happy and healthy. In order to keep your Mini Lop Rabbit healthy, you need to make sure it is healthy even before you bring it home.

Many inexperienced rabbit owners make the mistake of not taking the time to carefully select a breeder and to examine the rabbit before buying to make sure it is in good condition. In this section you will learn how to choose a reputable breeder and how to then pick out a healthy rabbit.

Follow these tips to make sure you bring home a healthy Mini Lop Rabbit:

- Do your research before picking a breeder and buying a rabbit

- Take a tour of the facilities

- Observe and examine the rabbit kits individually

- Make your choice and start the process

Do your research.

Shop around for a reputable breeder and take the time to interview each breeder. Ask questions to ascertain the breeder's knowledge of and experience with the Mini Lop Breed. If the breeder can't answer your questions or appears to be avoiding them, move on to another breeder.

Ask for a tour.

Once you select a breeder, pay a visit to the facilities. Ask to see the places where the rabbits are kept and ask to see the parents of the litter from which you are buying. If the facilities are dirty or the parents appear to be in poor health, do not purchase a rabbit from that breeder.

Observe the kits.

If the facilities and parents appear to be in good order, ask to see the litter of rabbits. Observe their appearance and activity to see if they look healthy. Healthy Mini Lops should be active and curious, not hiding in a corner or acting lethargic.

Examine the rabbits individually.

If the litter appears to be in good condition, pick out a few of the rabbits that you like. Having got permission, handle the rabbits briefly to see how they react to human interaction and check them for obvious signs of disease and injury. Check the rabbit's ears and nose for discharge and make sure that the eyes are bright and clear. The rabbit's teeth should be straight and its coat healthy.

If, after touring the facilities and ensuring that the rabbits themselves are healthy, you can begin negotiations with the breeder. Make sure you get the rabbit's medical history and breeding information for your own records. Ask if the rabbit comes with a health guarantee and make sure you get all the paperwork necessary to register your rabbit, should you choose to do so.

Chapter Five: Caring for Mini Lop Rabbits

1) Habitat Requirements

Mini Lop Rabbits are not a very high-maintenance breed but there are a few basic things you need to provide. One of the most important needs you must meet for your rabbit is the requirement for shelter. Many rabbit owners choose to let their rabbits roam free in the house (especially if they are litter trained) but it is still strongly recommended that you have a rabbit cage where you can keep your rabbit safe at night or when you have left the home. In this chapter you will find all the information you need to help you pick the right cage for your Mini Lop Rabbit.

a) Picking a Rabbit Cage

Your Mini Lop Rabbit is going to spend a significant amount of time in this cage so it is essential that you pick a good one. Though these rabbits do remain fairly small, they still need to have plenty of space in their cage. A cage for Mini Lops should be long enough that your rabbit can make three or four hops from one end to the other. The cage should be wide enough that your rabbit can stretch out across the width and tall enough that it can stand on its hind legs.

An open exercise pen or rabbit run can be as large as you like but the walls should be at least 3 feet (91.4 cm) high so your bunny doesn't escape. You may also want to bury the wire at least a few inches underground to prevent your rabbit from digging under it. I strongly recommend that you also make sure the top of the pen is covered so predators cannot get in to attack your rabbit. Another thing you need to think about when keeping your rabbit in an exercise pen outdoors is that you should cover about half of the pen with a towel or another solid object to provide your rabbit with shade.

In addition to the size, you also need to think about the materials from which your rabbit cage is built. Metal cages made from wire mesh with a solid bottom are best. Cages that have wire mesh bottoms may make clean-up easier by allowing feces to fall through the holes, but it can also hurt your rabbit's feet. It is far better to clean out your rabbit's cage often enough that the bedding remains fresh.

In terms of bedding, the best kinds to use are non-toxic pelleted litter, fresh hay or newspaper. Pine and cedar shavings can cause irritation and both clay and clumping cat litters can be harmful to rabbits. You should also avoid using colored magazine pages as bedding because the ink on the pages may be toxic – it could be dangerous for your rabbit if he eats it.

b) Benefits of Multi-Level Cages

In addition to deciding whether you want to keep your rabbit indoors or outdoors, you also need to think about what kind of cage you want to provide it with. Indoor cages come in two main varieties: single-level and multi-level. Multi-level cages are also referred to as rabbit condos and they provide vertical space as well as horizontal space.

The main difference between these two options is the

amount of space they provide. With a single-level cage, the only way to provide more space is to increase the length and width dimensions of the cage – the larger the cage, the more space it takes up in your house. A multi-level cage on the other hand, provides extra space by adding different levels. You can arrange your multi-level cage so that the litter pan is on the bottom with the food with resting and playing areas on the upper floors.

No matter which option you choose, you should also think about how you are going to provide your rabbit with free space. Ideally, your rabbit should only spend a few hours a day (most likely at night) in his cage – the rest of the time he should be allowed to roam freely or given time in an open enclosure or rabbit run. To build your own rabbit run, all you need are a few interlocking mesh panels. You can also build a wooden frame and cover the sides with wire mesh. As already mentioned, if you use your rabbit run outdoors, be sure to provide your rabbits with an area of shade.

c) Keeping Your Rabbit Indoors vs. Outdoors

Whether you keep your Mini Lop Rabbit indoors or outdoors is your choice, but I've summarized the pros and cons of both options to help you make a decision. There is no right or wrong answer but what suits you and your circumstances best:

Pros for Indoor Rabbits

- More likely to receive adequate attention and interaction with human caregivers

- Not exposed to inclement weather or predators

- Less likely to come into contact with parasites

- Longer lifespan, less susceptible to disease

- More likely to form a bond with owners

Cons for Indoor Rabbits

- Noise and odor which is more noticeable if cage isn't cleaned often enough

- Cage takes up space in the home

- Free-roaming rabbits may be underfoot or escape and could potentially be injured

- Free-roaming rabbits may chew on electrical cords, furniture, etc.

Pros for Outdoor Rabbits

- Clean-up can be much easier, may not even need to litter train rabbits

- Easier to accommodate large cages and multiple rabbits

- Noise and odor are not an issue although the cage must still be cleaned regularly
- More space for rabbits to stretch out and exercise

- May supplement their diet by eating grass and other plants in the yard (if free roaming) although this can be a con as well if the plants are toxic or if you use pesticides which can be harmful to your rabbit

Cons for Outdoor Rabbits

- May be exposed to inclement weather and extreme temperatures

- More likely to be exposed to parasites and other dangerous diseases

- May be less likely to form a bond with human caretakers and pets

- At risk of attack by predators

- Rabbits may not receive as much human interaction

- Cannot monitor what they are eating as easily and could expose your rabbit to toxic substances

d) Toys and Cage Accessories

Rabbits do not require a great many accessories for their cages. The basic necessities include:

- Water Bottle

- Food Bowl(s)

- Hay Compartment

- Litter Pan

- Chew Toys

- Nest Box or Shelter

- Other Toys

Toys for Mini Lop Rabbits do not need to be extravagant – they do not even need to be store-bought! You can make your own rabbit toys at home out of cardboard tubes, boxes, plastic balls, wooden blocks and whatever else you have on hand! Please ensure that any materials used are non-toxic and BPA free.

2) Feeding Mini Lop Rabbits

Along with plenty of attention, perhaps the most important factor in maintaining your Mini Lop Rabbit's health is offering him a healthy diet. A diet for rabbits should be high in fiber and relatively low in calories – primarily made up of hay and grass which should help keep their digestive system working happily and also to keep their teeth nice and trimmed down.

Before you go out and buy food for your rabbit, take some time to learn about your rabbit's nutritional needs and what you can do to meet them every day.

a) Nutritional Needs

In addition to hay, ensure your rabbit is given some fresh food daily with the bulk of it being made up of leafy greens with varied textures and tastes such as Carrot tops, Cucumber leaves, Kale, Spring greens, Turnip greens, Dandelion greens, Mint, Basil, Watercress, Chicory, Wheatgrass, Bok Choy, Fennel (the leafy tops as well as the base), Borage leaves and Dill leaves. Occasional servings of Parsley, Spinach, Mustard greens, Beet greens, Swiss chard and Radish tops in addition to those above are also fine.

Mini Lop Rabbits require a diet that is low in protein and high in fiber. The majority of your rabbit's additional diet should be made up of high-quality feed, also called pellets but should only form a small percentage of their overall daily intake. Do not just grab a bag of rabbit pellets off the shelf – not all rabbit pellets are created equal. It is important that you take the time to review the ingredients list on the package to determine whether it is a good quality food to offer your rabbit. Ideally, rabbit pellets should contain no more than 16% protein and at least 15% to 20% fiber.

The main ingredient in your rabbit's pellets should be alfalfa – if it is first on the ingredients list that means it is the main ingredient by concentration. If you purchase a low-quality feed, you may be purchasing a produce that consists mainly of feed dust or one that contains artificial "binders". You should also be sure that the feed is free from corn and growth hormones.

When reading the food labels on your rabbit's pellets, you should look to determine what type of grain is used. The two most commonly used grains in rabbit pellets are oats and barley. Corn is not ideal, though very small amounts in the feed are unlikely to cause any negative effects. Many Mini Lops prefer oat formulas over barley formulas but your rabbit's preferences may be different. If you want to try out different types of feed, be sure to make the transition slowly so it doesn't upset your rabbit's stomach.

b) How Much to Feed

How much you feed your Mini Lop Rabbit will vary depending on its age and size. Baby rabbits that have just been weaned, which is about 6 weeks, can be given unlimited access to pellets until they reach 6 months of age. During this time you can also offer baby rabbits Timothy hay. It is not a good idea however, to give your baby rabbits too many vegetables because it can upset their delicate stomachs.

Once your rabbit reaches 6 months of age you can begin feeding it a limited amount of rabbit feed. Mini Lop Rabbits should be fed 0.75 to 1 oz. (21.3 to 28.3 g) of feed per pound of body weight. If you Mini Lops weighs 6 lbs. (2.72 kg) this means they need about 4.5 to 6 oz. (127.8 to 169.8 g) of feed per day.

You may choose whether you want to offer all of your rabbit's food at once or if you want to divide it into two or more separate feedings, which if possible is recommended. In addition to the pellets, you should also make sure your rabbits have an unlimited supply of Timothy hay and fresh water. Don't be too worried about getting the amount of pellets exactly right for if your rabbits are still hungry, they will always have hay to eat and if they are given too much food, they do not have to eat the extra.

c) Types of Food

In addition to commercial rabbit pellets, you can also feed your rabbits some fresh fruits and vegetables. Be careful, however, because offering rabbits too much can be detrimental, especially to young rabbits whose stomachs are still sensitive.

Avoid feeding your Mini Lop Rabbit the following vegetables:

- Corn

- Iceberg Lettuce

- Peas

- Pennyroyal Mint

- Potatoes

**Note: You should also limit the amount of spinach and celery you offer your rabbits because these foods are lower in nutritional content than other vegetables. I would recommend that you check with your veterinarian or breeder before introducing any new foods to your rabbit that they have not previously recommended.

Food Safe for Rabbits

Apples	Orange
Beans	Pear
Blueberries	Papaya
Carrots	Pineapple
Cherries	Peach
Dandelion Greens	Peas
Grapes	Parsnip
Kale	Parsley
Mustard Greens	Raspberries
Mango	Strawberries
Melon	Tomatoes (fruit)

Plants Toxic to Rabbits

There are some plants that are considered toxic to rabbits and they include:

Acorns	Juniper
Aloe	Jack-in-the-Pulpit
Apple Seeds	Laurel Lupine
Almonds	Lily of the Valley
Asparagus Fern	Marigold
Azalea	Milkweed
Carnations	Mistletoe
Clematis	Nutmeg
Daffodil Bulbs	Oak
Eucalyptus	Parsnip
Fruit Pits	Poppy
Fruit Seeds	Peony
Geranium	Philodendron
Gladiola	Poinsettia
Hemlock	Rhubarb Leaves
Hyacinth Bulbs	Sweet Potato
Impatiens	Tansy
Iris	Tomato Leaves
Ivy	Tulip Bulbs
Jasmine	Violet
Jessamine	Yew

*This list is not comprehensive; in order to determine whether a specific plant is toxic for rabbits, consult the House Rabbit Society website:
http://rabbit.org/poisonous-plants/

d) Tips for Feeding Mini Lop Rabbits

- Choose a certain time of day to feed your rabbits or divide their food into two daily meals (rabbits appreciate routine)

- Make any dietary changes slowly – drastic changes in feed can cause severe digestive problems

- Always use pellets within 60 days of manufacture (not purchase)

- Check your feed often for signs of mold or foul odor – these signs indicate that the feed has gone bad

- Trust your rabbits – if they suddenly stop eating the feed there may be something wrong with it and you should remove it immediately

- If they stop eating and it isn't the food, they may be ill, so watch them carefully and take them to the vet if you are concerned

- Always keep an unlimited supply of fresh water available for your rabbits – dehydration can cause severe health problems

- Avoid commercially produced rabbit treats because they are rarely healthy

3) Litter Training Your Mini Lop Rabbit

In many cases, rabbits will litter train themselves because they are naturally clean animals. If you do need to litter train your rabbit, however, it is not difficult to do. You will need to start by isolating your rabbit in a small area without carpeting or wooden floors as this will make it easier to clean up any mess.

Next, prepare a litter box that is large enough for your rabbit to lie down in. Fill the litter box with about 1 inch (2.54 cm) of non-toxic litter and cover it with a layer of hay. Take some of the soiled hay from your rabbit's cage add it to the litter box to encourage your rabbit to use it. Shoo it towards the box when you see it eliminating and reward your rabbit when successful but never scold after the fact!

Another option is to place multiple litter boxes in your rabbit's cage. Keep an eye on your rabbit and take note of which areas he tends to choose to do his business. Keep the litter boxes in those areas and remove the rest. Your rabbit might have a few accidents outside the litter box now and then but this is normal behavior.

Note: Certain types of litter are harmful to Mini Lop Rabbits including clay litter, clumping litter, pine or cedar shavings and corn cob litter.

Chapter Six: Keeping Healthy

** **Note:** This section may be upsetting to any children who read it. Sadly like all our pets, Mini Lop Rabbits are susceptible to developing certain health issues.

In order to keep your Mini Lop Rabbit happy and healthy, you need to keep its cage clean and offer it a varied, high-quality diet. You should familiarize yourself with some of the diseases most commonly affecting this breed.

If you know the symptoms and warning signs, you can quickly obtain a diagnosis and seek the proper treatment for your pet – the sooner you take action, the greater your rabbit's chances for making a full recovery.

1) Common Health Problems

The details in this section are not exhaustive and not designed to take the place of a qualified veterinarian who will have up to date knowledge and information regarding current treatments for any ailments. It is important to remember that although some health conditions affecting Mini Lop Rabbits can be treated at home, severe cases should always be examined by a veterinarian. If you are in any doubt or the disease is impacting your rabbit's health or mobility, do not delay in taking it to the vet.

Colibacillosis

Colibacillosis is characterized by severe diarrhea and it is often caused by *Escherichia coli*. This disease can be seen in two forms depending on the rabbit's age. Newborn rabbits may exhibit a yellowish diarrhea – in newborns, this condition is often fatal and can affect the entire litter. In weaned rabbits, the intestines may fill with fluid and hemorrhages may surface.

In the case of weaned rabbits, the disease is typically fatal within 2 weeks. If the rabbit survives, it is likely to be stunted. Treatment is not often successful but, in mild cases, antibiotics may help. Rabbits that are severely affected with this disease should be culled to avoid the spread of the disease.

Causes: *Escherichia coli*

Symptoms: yellowish diarrhea in newborns; fluid-filled intestines and hemorrhages in weaned rabbits

Treatment: antibiotics; treatment is not often effective

Dental Problems

All rabbits, including Mini Lop Rabbits, are prone to developing dental problems. The most common issues are overgrown molars and enamel spurs. Your rabbit's teeth may become overgrown or develop spurs if you don't provide enough fiber-rich foods. Fibrous foods are naturally abrasive which helps to keep your rabbit's teeth filed down. In most cases, dental problems require veterinary treatment.

Causes: *Diet too low in fiber*

Symptoms: overgrown molars, enamel spurs

Treatment: veterinary exam and treatment

Dermatophytosis

Also known as ringworm, Dermatophytosis is caused by either *Trichophyton mentagrophytes* or *Microsporum canis*. These infections typically result from poor husbandry or inadequate nutrition. Ringworm can be transmitted through direct contact with an infected rabbit or sharing tools such as brushes. The symptoms of ringworm include circular raised bumps on the body. The skin is these areas may be red and capped with a white, flaky material. Some of the most common treatments for ringworm include topical antifungal creams that contain miconazole or itraconazole. A 1% copper sulfate dip may also be effective.

Causes: *Trichophyton mentagrophytes or Microsporum canis;* typically results from poor husbandry or inadequate nutrition

Symptoms: circular raised bumps on the body; skin is red and capped with a white, flaky material

Treatment: include topical antifungal creams that contain miconazole or itraconazole; 1% copper sulfate dip

Enterotoxemia

Enterotoxemia is a disease characterized by explosive diarrhea and it typically affects rabbits between the ages of

4 and 8 weeks. Symptoms of this condition include lethargy, loss of condition and greenish-brown fecal matter around the perianal area. In many cases, this condition is fatal within 48 hours.

The primary cause of this disease is *Clostridium spiroforme*. These organisms are common in rabbits in small numbers but they can become a problem when the rabbit's diet is too low in fiber. Treatment may not be effective due to the rapid progression of the disease but adding cholestryamine or copper sulfate to the diet can help prevent enterotoxemia. Reducing stress in young rabbits and increasing fiber intake can also help.

Causes: *Clostridium spiroforme*

Symptoms: lethargy, loss of condition and greenish-brown fecal matter around the perianal area

Treatment: may not be effective; adding cholestryamine or copper sulfate to the diet can help prevent

<u>Fleas/Mites</u>

Indoor rabbits are unlikely to contract fleas and ticks on their own. If your rabbit spends time outside or if you have other pets that spend time outside, however, your rabbit could be at risk. Mites are typically found in the ears and fur of rabbits and they most often present themselves after your rabbit's immune system has already been compromised.

Fur mites tend to stay at the base of the neck or near the rabbit's rear. If left untreated, mites and fleas can cause severe itching, bald spots and bleeding. The best treatment for fleas and mites is a prescription medication called Revolution, known in the UK as Stronghold. Another treatment option in the UK is Ivermectin drops.

Causes: *Exposure to infested pets, spending time outside*

Symptoms: itching, bald spots, bleeding

Treatment: prescription medication; Revolution in the USA, known in the UK as Stronghold or Ivermectin drops.

Listeriosis

Listeriosis is a type of sporadic septicemia which often causes sudden death or abortion – this condition is most common in pregnant Does. Some of the contributing factors for this disease include poor husbandry and stress. Some of the common symptoms include anorexia, depression and weight loss.

If not properly treated, the *Listeria monocytogenes* responsible for the disease can spread to the blood, liver and uterus. Treatment is not often attempted because diagnosis is not frequently made premortem.

Causes: *Listeria monocytogenes*

Symptoms: anorexia, depression and weight loss; often causes sudden death or abortion

Treatment: not often attempted because diagnosis is not frequently made premortem

Mastitis

This condition is most commonly seen in rabbitries but it can affect single rabbits. Mastitis is a condition that affects pregnant Does and it is caused by *Staphylococci* bacteria. The bacteria infect the mammary glands, causing them to become hot, red and swollen. If the disease is allowed to progress, it may cause septicemia and become fatal.

Does affected by mastitis are unlikely to eat but they will crave water. The rabbit may also run a fever. Treatment for this condition may include antibiotic treatment. Penicillin, however, should be avoided because it can cause diarrhea. Kits should not be fostered because they will only end up spreading the disease.

Causes: *Staphylococci bacteria*

Symptoms: hot, red and swollen mammary glands; loss of appetite; fever

Treatment: antibiotics

Myxomatosis

Myxomatosis is a viral disease that is caused by *Myxoma* virus. This condition is typically fatal and it can be transmitted through direct contact or through biting insects. Some of the initial symptoms of the disease include conjunctivitis, eye discharge, listlessness, anorexia and fever. In severe cases, death may occur after only 48 hours.

Treatment for this condition is generally not effective and it can cause severe and lasting damage. A vaccine is available to be given after the rabbit reaches 6 weeks of age.

Causes*: Myxoma virus; transmitted through direct contact or through biting insects*

Symptoms: conjunctivitis, eye discharge, listlessness, anorexia and fever

Treatment: generally not effective; vaccine is available

Otitis Media

Also called "wry neck" or "head tilt," otitis media is caused by an infection resulting from *P multocida* or *Encephalitozoon cunuculi*. These bacteria cause the accumulation of fluid or pus in the ear, causing the rabbit to tilt its head. Antibiotic therapy may be effective, though it may just worsen the condition. In most cases, rabbits infected with this condition are culled.

Causes: *P multocida or Encephalitozoon cunuculi bacteria*

Symptoms: accumulation of fluid or pus in the ear, causing the rabbit to tilt its head

Treatment: antibiotic therapy may be effective

Papillomatosis

Papillomatosis is fairly common in domestic rabbits and it is caused by the *rabbit oral papillomavirus*. This disease results in the formation of small grey nodules or warts on the underside of the tongue or floor of the mouth. Another type, caused by *cottontail papillomavirus*, may produce horned warts on the neck, shoulders, ears and abdomen. There is no treatment for these conditions but the lesions typically go away on their own in time.

Causes: *Rabbit oral papillomavirus, cottontail papillomavirus*

Symptoms: small grey nodules or warts on the underside of the tongue or floor of the mouth or horned warts on the neck, shoulders, ears and abdomen

Treatment: no treatment; the lesions typically go away on their own in time

Parasites

One of the most common parasites found in rabbits is *Encephalitozoon cuniculi*. This protozoan parasite can survive in the body for years without causing any harm. In some cases, however, the parasite can cause severe damage. This parasite typically causes nerve damage which results in head tilting, incontinence, paralysis and rupture of the lens of the eye.

Intestinal worms are also a common problem in rabbits. Both of these conditions can be treated with de-worming paste. This treatment can be used for infected rabbits and as a preventive against parasites. When used as a preventive, the paste is typically administered twice a year.

Causes: *Encephalitozoon cuniculi, intestinal worms*

Symptoms: head tilting, incontinence, paralysis and rupture of the lens of the eye

Treatment: de-worming paste

Pneumonia

Pneumonia is fairly common in domestic rabbits and it is most often a secondary infection. The most common cause of pneumonia in rabbits is *P multocida* bacteria, though other kinds may be involved. A precursor of pneumonia is often upper respiratory disease which may be a result of inadequate ventilation or sanitation.

Some of the common symptoms of pneumonia include listlessness, fever and anorexia. Once they show symptoms, most rabbits succumb to the infection within 1 week. Though antibiotic treatment is often used, it is not typically effective because it may not be administered until the disease is highly advanced.

Causes: *P multocida bacteria*

Symptoms: listlessness, fever and anorexia

Treatment: antibiotic treatment is often used but not typically effective

Rhinitis

Rhinitis is the medical term used to describe sniffling or chronic inflammation in the airway and lungs. This condition is often caused by *Pastuerella*, though *Staphylococcus* or *Streptococcus* may also be involved. The initial symptom of this disease is a thin stream of mucus flowing from the nose. As the disease progresses, the flow may encrust the fur on the paws and chest. Sneezing and coughing may also be exhibited. This condition generally resolves itself but even recovered rabbits can be carriers of the disease.

Causes: *Is often caused by Pastuerella, though Staphylococcus or Streptococcus may also be involved*

Symptoms: sniffling or chronic inflammation in the airway and lungs; thin stream of mucus flowing from the nose

Treatment: generally resolves itself

<u>Uterine Cancer</u>

A common cause of death in female rabbits, uterine cancer can easily be prevented. Spaying female rabbits between the ages of 5 months and 2 years is the best way to prevent this disease. In un-spayed female rabbits, uterine cancer can spread to several different organs before the disease is diagnosed. At that point, treatment is typically ineffective.

Causes: *Tumor growing in the uterus*

Symptoms: other reproductive issues; endometriosis, bulging veins, vaginal discharge, bloody urine

Treatment: spaying female rabbits to prevent; once the cancer develops, treatment is generally ineffective

Viral Hemorrhagic Disease

Also called rabbit hemorrhagic disease, viral hemorrhagic disease is caused by *Rabbit calcivirus* transmitted through direct contact or contaminated food, water and bedding. Unfortunately, there is no effective treatment for this condition and many rabbits die from it without ever showing symptoms.

Some of the most common symptoms of viral hemorrhagic disease include difficulty breathing, paralysis, lethargy, bloody discharge from the nose, weight loss and convulsions. Once symptoms appear, the disease is typically fatal within 2 weeks.

Causes: *Rabbit calcivirus; transmitted through direct contact or contaminated food, water and bedding*

Symptoms: difficulty breathing, paralysis, lethargy, bloody discharge from the nose, weight loss and convulsions

Treatment: no effective treatment

Wool Block

All breeds are prone to developing a dangerous condition called Wool Block although it is most prevalent in wooly breeds. Wool Block occurs when a ball of hair forms in the stomach and intestines of the rabbit, preventing it from digesting any food. This can lead to inadequate nutrition and eventual starvation and death.

Rabbits are incapable of vomiting to clear the hairball. It is recommended that you speak to your breeder before purchasing your rabbit as some people feel that a pre-disposition to wool block can be inherited. You can check with your breeder whether it is a problem that they have experienced with their stock.

There are several things that you can do to help prevent and diagnose wool block. Your rabbit must have access to fresh de-chlorinated water at all times and should have lots of exercise. It is essential that your rabbit is fed with a diet that is high in fiber and contains plenty of hay. Many owners supplement with papaya tablets or fresh papaya or pineapple chunks once a week as the enzymes in these help dissolve the food within the fiber and therefore allow it to be passed more easily through the intestines. Other owners will on one day each week feed their rabbit hay and two tablespoons of whole oats and/or extra fresh vegetables. On this day, they do not feed their rabbit any pellets, allowing their stomach an opportunity to clean out. You should also ensure that your rabbit is groomed properly to reduce the amount of hair that they ingest.

Additionally you should study their droppings each day and become familiar with what is normal for your rabbit and note any changes. Droppings that become smaller or are a string of beads mixed with hair, can be a sign of wool block. Due to the seriousness of this condition, if you are in any doubt, you should seek veterinarian advice immediately.

Causes: *Ball of hair in the stomach and intestines*

Symptoms: Changes in eating patterns, weight loss, change in droppings, lethargy

Treatment: Seek veterinarian attention as opinions vary on treatment

2) Preventing Illness

There are several things you can do to help protect your rabbit against disease. The most important thing is to provide your rabbit with a clean, healthy environment. It is essential that you clean your rabbit's cage on a regular basis and provide plenty of fresh de-chlorinated water for him to drink. You should also be sure to provide a healthy, varied diet that meets all of your rabbit's nutritional needs.

a) Dangerous/Toxic Foods

There are certain foods and plants which can be very harmful for your Mini Lop Rabbit. Please refer to the list of foods that can cause serious problems in the Feeding Mini Lop Rabbits section in Chapter Five. You can also check with your vet or local breeder on any local foodstuffs that you might consider feeding your rabbit to avoid heartache.

b) Recommended Vaccinations

Having your rabbit vaccinated is one of the best things you can do to protect it from disease. Two of the most important vaccines for Mini Lop Rabbits are against myxomatosis and viral hemorrhagic disease (VHD) – both of these vaccinations are highly recommended.

These vaccines are available as single vaccines, which need to be taken nine days apart every six months, or as a single combined vaccine once a year. The recommended vaccines for your rabbit will depend on where you live and your vet can advise you what is required.

It is a good idea to have your rabbit examined as soon as possible by a vet after you bring it home. Your vet will be able to assess your rabbit's condition and set a schedule for future check-ups. Additionally, your vet will also offer recommendations on what vaccines your pet needs and how often he needs them. This will vary from area to area so getting up to date local knowledge is essential.

It may seem like a needless cost to take your rabbit to the vet once a year but it can save you a lot of money and heartache in diagnosing serious diseases before they become untreatable.

c) Ears, Eyes, Nails and Teeth

In addition to vaccinating your rabbit you should also check its condition on your own from time to time. Take a look inside your rabbit's ears for signs of wax buildup or infection – unpleasant odor may also be a sign of infection. Your rabbit's feet should be dry and free from sores. If you notice patches of skin where the fur has worn away or swelling, you should seek immediate veterinary care.

When petting your rabbit, take the time to check its skin and coat. If you notice white flakes or tiny white dots, your rabbit could have mites or fleas.

A rabbit's nails grow continuously so you will need to trim them every six to eight weeks. Trimming your rabbit's nails is not a difficult task but it does require a degree of caution. Inside your rabbit's nail lies the quick – a vein which supplies blood to the nail. If you cut your rabbit's nails too short, you could sever the quick and induce severe bleeding. When clipping your rabbit's nails it is best to only cut off the pointed tip. To be safe, have your veterinarian show you how to properly trim a rabbit's nails before you try it yourself.

One of the most common causes of runny eyes in rabbits is a bacterial eye infection. These infections can be very dangerous and must be treated by a veterinarian as soon as possible. In many cases, antibiotics will be prescribed to handle the infection.

Obstructions and inflammation in the eye may be the result of natural or unnatural causes. In some cases, a piece of bedding or some other object may get stuck in the eye causing it to water or become inflamed. It is also possible, however, for a misshapen eyelid or part of the bone in the rabbit's face to cause an obstruction. If the flow of tears is obstructed, they may form a path down the cheek, discoloring the fur. Depending on the cause of the obstruction, surgery may be necessary to correct the issue.

If the rabbit's eyes do not produce enough tears on their own, they may become dry and irritated. When the eyes become too dry, they are more prone to scratches and erosions which can have a devastating effect on your rabbit's ability to see properly. Some of the symptoms of dry eyes include squinting, eye discharge, redness and inflammation. Trauma to the eye can also interfere with the production of tears and should be evaluated by a veterinarian.

Depending what type of litter you use in your rabbit's cage, your rabbit could develop watery eyes as a result of allergies. Dust from the litter, hay or food in your rabbit's cage can get into the eyes and cause irritation. To prevent this from happening, choose litter that is dust-free and make sure the cage is well ventilated.

If your rabbit's teeth are not properly aligned they can develop a condition called malocclusion. There are three main causes of this, the most common being genetic predisposition, injury or bacterial infection. If you provide your rabbit with adequate chew toys, you shouldn't have to worry about its teeth becoming overgrown.

You should, however, make frequent checks to see if the teeth are properly aligned – if they aren't, your rabbit could develop molar spurs or abscesses in the mouth.

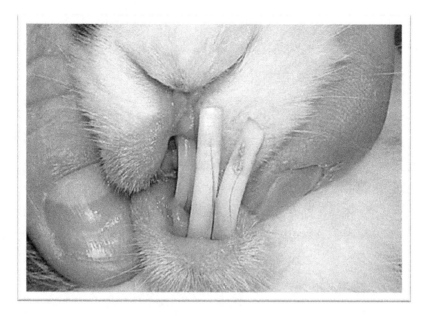

*In some rabbits, the teeth are not properly aligned,
a condition called malocclusion.*

3) Pet Insurance

Many pet owners have discovered that pet insurance helps defray the costs of veterinary expenses. Pet insurance is similar to health insurance in that you pay a monthly premium and a deductible (excess in the UK) and the pet insurance pays for whatever is covered in your plan and can include annual exams and blood work. Shopping for pet insurance is similar to shopping for health insurance in the United States. As with health insurance, the age and the overall health of your rabbit will determine how much you will pay in premiums and deductibles.

Ask plenty of questions to determine the best company and plan for your needs. Some of the questions that you should ask are:

- Can you go to your regular vet, or do you have to go to a vet assigned by the pet insurance company?

- What does the insurance plan cover? Does it cover annual exams? Surgeries? Emergency illness and injury?

- Does coverage begin immediately?

- Are pre-existing conditions covered? In addition, if your rabbit develops a health issue and you later have to renew the policy, is that condition covered when you renew your policy?

- Is medication covered?

- Do you have to have pre-authorization before your pet receives treatment? What happens if your rabbit has the treatment without pre-authorization?

- Is there a lifetime maximum benefit amount? If so, how much is that amount?

Take the time to research your pet insurance options. Compare the different plans available, what each covers, and the cost before making the decision on which is best for you and your pet. Of course, pet insurance may not be the answer for everyone.

While pet insurance may not be a feasible option for you, consider having a backup plan, just in case your rabbit requires emergency care or you run into unexpected veterinarian costs.

A simple way to prepare for an emergency is to start a veterinary fund for your rabbit. Decide to put a certain amount of money aside each week, each month, or each paycheck to use in the case of an emergency. Think about the potential financial costs of veterinary care and plan for how you will pay for it now instead of waiting until something occurs.

4) Planning for the Unexpected

If something happens to you, you want to know that your rabbit and any other pets will be properly cared for and loved. Some cell phones allow you to input an ICE (In Case of Emergency) number with notes. If your cell phone has such an option, use it. If it does not, write the following information on a piece of a paper and put it in your wallet with your driver's license:

- The names of each of your pets, including your rabbit.

- The names and phone numbers of family members or friends who have agreed to temporarily care for your pets in an emergency.

- The name and phone number of your veterinarian.

Be sure to also talk with your neighbors, letting them know how many pets you have and the type of pets. That way, if something happens to you, they can alert the authorities, ensuring your pets do not linger for days before they are found.

If you fail to do that and something happens to you, someone will find your rabbit and any other pets and will need to know what to do to ensure that they are cared for. It is a good idea in the case of an emergency, to ask several friends or family members to be responsible for taking care of your pets should something happen to you.

Prepare instructions for the intended guardians, providing amended instructions as necessary. Also, be sure to provide each individual with a key to your home (remember to inform your home insurance company so that this does not affect your coverage). Instructions should include:

- The name and phone numbers of each individual who agreed to take care of your rabbit and other pets.

- Your pet's diet and feeding schedule.

- The name and phone number of your veterinarian.

- Any health problems and medications your rabbit may take on a daily basis, including dosage instructions, instructions on how to give the medicine, and where the medicine is kept.

Put as much information as necessary to ensure the guardians can provide the same level of care to which your rabbit is accustomed.

Chapter Seven: Breeding Mini Lop Rabbits

The following is intended as a broad overview only. If you decide to move forward with the breeding of rabbits, you will need to conduct extensive research in the process and make sure that you have all the necessary supplies on hands. Little lives will be depending on you!

1) Basic Breeding Information

As you learned in the beginning of this book, a female Mini Lop Rabbit is called a Doe and a male is a Buck. Breeding is the process through which a male and female rabbit are mated in order to produce a litter of kits (babies). Female Mini Lop Rabbits typically reach sexual maturity around the age of 5 to 6 months while males may take a little longer, reaching maturity between 7 and 8 months of age.

After a Buck and a Doe have been mated, ideally, the female rabbit will become pregnant. At this point, she will enter a period of gestation – this is the length of time it takes for the babies to develop. For Mini Lop Rabbits, the gestation period typically lasts about 31 days. At the end of the gestation period the Doe will give birth to her kits in a process called kindling.

Once the kits have been born, the Dam (mother rabbit) will care for them. The kits will receive nutrition from their mother's milk, nursing for the next few weeks until they are old enough to be weaned. During the last two weeks of the gestation period and while your Doe is lactating, it is important that you provide her with a healthy diet higher in protein than her normal diet – this will enable her to produce enough milk to feed her kits.

2) The Breeding Process

Before you introduce your male and female rabbits to each other, you need to be sure they are both healthy and of good breeding age. Mini Lop Rabbits tend to prefer breeding in the morning and evening, so these are the best times to attempt a mating. Ideally, the female rabbit should be brought into the male rabbit's cage rather than the other way around. If you put the male in the female's cage, he may be too distracted by the strange environment to mate.

Once the Doe is ready for mating, she will stretch herself out and raise her tail. It should not take long for the male to climb on and the mating process itself takes only a few seconds. You do not need to remove the female rabbit immediately – wait a few minutes to see if the two breed again. Multiple sessions can increase the chance of pregnancy and may also increase the size of the litter.

After conception has occurred, the gestation period lasts about 31 days. Around day 26 or 27 it is a good idea to set up a nest box in the cage. The female rabbit will line the nest box with hay in preparation for kindling and may also pull out some of her own fur to line the nest. To build your own nest box for your Mini Lop Rabbits, just construct a simple plywood box 10 x 10 x 10 inches (25.4 x 25.4 x 25.4 cm). If you are worried about the temperature in your home, you might want to place a specialist heat lamp about 12 inches (30.5 cm) over the box to keep your kits warm. Heat lamps with thermostats are available in a price range of $35 to $50 (£22.75 to £32.50) with replacement bulbs averaging $10 to $15 (£6.50 to £9.75). Ensure that you get a specialist heat lamp to reduce the risk of fire.

After 29 to 31 days, the Doe will be ready to give birth. Once the birthing process begins, it typically only takes 20 minutes. Mini Lop Rabbits generally have litters of 2 to 4 kits, though new mothers may have fewer. It is not uncommon for small breeds to produce stillborn kits, particularly during a first breeding. The Doe may wait a few hours after birth to feed the kits, so do not be alarmed.

You should check the babies after birth and remove any stillborn kits. After that, leave the babies alone for at least the first day so as not to agitate the mother.

3) Raising the Babies

Once the babies have been born, the Doe will do all of the work caring for her kits. The most important aspect in caring for newborn kits is to make sure they stay warm. Sometimes new mothers will give birth to their kits outside the nest box – it is essential that you move them carefully to the nest box so they stay warm. After doing so, do not touch or move the babies for at least a day or two.

In most cases, the Dam will start feeding her babies after a few hours. Do not be worried if you don't see her feeding the kits because baby rabbits only need to feed for a few minutes each day. Generally, feedings are done in the early morning or evening when you may not be around anyway. In case you don't see the babies feeding, check the shape of their bodies to see if they are being fed. Well-fed babies should have rounded bellies that puff out to the sides.

When the baby rabbits are first born they will be blind, deaf and hairless. After a day or two, they will begin to develop a layer of fuzz which will help keep them warm. After about 10 days the kits should open their eyes and their ears should come up as well. Do not be worried if the ears do not appear to be lopped – it can take several months (or even years) for this to happen. After about 3 weeks, the babies generally start to sample solid food and they should be completely weaned around 5 to 6 weeks of age.

Once the kits are weaned it is best to remove the mother from the cage. You can continue to keep the kits together for another few weeks but separate them when they reach 2 months old. Though most Mini Lops do not become sexually mature until 5 or 6 months of age, some do sooner. Young Bucks may also start fighting at which point it is recommended that you separate them.

Chapter Eight: Showing Mini Lop Rabbits

1) Breed Standard

The Mini Lop breed standard used by the American Rabbit Breeders Association adds up to a total of 100 points. The general type of the rabbit is evaluated out of 80 points while the fur is scored out of 10 points. The color and condition are scored out of 5 points each. A breakdown of the standard of points is as follows:

General Type – 80 points

Body (43 points)

Head (20 points)

Ears/Crown (12 points)

Feet, Legs and Bone (5 points)

Fur – 10 points

Color/Markings – 5 points

Condition – 5 points

Total Points = 100 points possible

The Mini Lop breed standard used by the British Rabbit Council (which recognizes the breed as the Dwarf Lop) adds up to a total of 100 points.

The general type and condition of the rabbit is evaluated out of 30 points while the coat (including guard hairs and color) is scored out of 45 points. The head, including the ears and eyes, is scored out of 25 points. A breakdown of the standard of points is as follows:

General Type and Condition – 30 points

Head, Ears, Crown and Eyes – 25 points

Coat – 20 points

Guard Hairs – 10 points

Color – 15 points

Total Points = 100 points possible

2) What to Know Before Showing

Before you attempt to show your Mini Lop Rabbit you should be very familiar with the breed standard to be sure your rabbit qualifies. Both the ARBA and the BRC provide complete copies of the breed standard on their websites that you can peruse.

Below you will find several key things to look for when assessing your rabbit's qualifications for show:

The show standards as defined by the ARBA in the U.S.A. for the Mini Lop are briefly summarized as follows -

Weight = Weight limits and showroom classes are as follows –

Senior Bucks (6 months of age or older) = 4.5 to 6.5 lbs. (2.04 to 2.95 kg)

Senior Does (6 months or older) = 3 to 6 lbs. (1.36 to 2.72 kg)

Junior Bucks or Does (under 6 months) = 3 to 6 lbs. (1.36 to 2.72 kg)

Type = massive, thick set, heavily muscled body

- Good balance of width and depth

- Slight taper from hind quarters to shoulders

- Good top line with peak over center of hips

- Hips smooth, deep, well rounded and full in the lower hips

- Legs should be straight, short and thick

Head, Crown, Ears and Eyes = head strong with bold features

- Neck as short as possible

- Crown of head boldly arched

- Should appear wide and have a well filled muzzle

- Size of head should balance with body

- Ears should give a horseshoe appearance

- Ears lie close to the cheeks with ear openings turned towards the head

- Ear length should be between ¾ and 1 inch (1.91 and 2.54 cm.) below the jaw, balanced with animal's size and be rounded on the ends and well-furred.

- Eyes may be any color but must match

Coat = fur is very thick and dense

- Should be glossy and lustrous

- Medium in length with good roll back

Colors = Please see the ARBA website for more information

Faults = long, narrow body

- Chopped or undercut in the hips and flat shoulders or hips

- Long narrow head, pointed nose, concave or flat crown

- Poor ear carriage, folds in ear, extremely thin or thick ears

- Ears turning away from the head

- Unmatched nails in broken colors

- General toenail disqualifications apply on all solid
  pattern groups

- Long, thin, silky, harsh or extremely short fur

- Lacking complete head markings, light body
  markings and excessive white hairs in a solid pattern

- Eyes that do not match are a disqualification as are
  foreign color spots in rabbits of the solid pattern
  group

**The show standards as defined by the BRC in the U.K. for
the Dwarf Lop are briefly summarized as follows -**

Weight = limits in the U.K. are between 4 lbs 4 oz. and 5 lbs.
4 oz. (1.93 to 2.38 kg).

Type = short body with well-rounded loins

- Chest is deep, shoulders wide
- Overall cobby, well-muscled appearance
- Legs are short and strong

Head, Crown, Ears and Eyes = well developed

- Eyes are wide-set, round and bright
- Cheeks are full, muzzle broad

- Crown is prominent across top of skull
- Ears are broad and thickly furred, rounded at ends
- Ears carried close to the cheek

Coat = dense and of good length

- Shows an abundance of guard hairs

Condition = perfect state of health

- Free from soiling on all body parts
- Coat reflects good overall health

Colors = Please see the BRC website for more information

Faults (loss of points)

- Body too long, shoulders too narrow
- Excessive white hairs in colored rabbits
- Ears are carried back or not lopped
- Light soiling on the feet, ears and genitals
- Fur is slightly soiled or matted
- Coat too short or fly-back
- Light or white tails in sooty fawns

Disqualifications

- Mutilated or maloccluded teeth
- Outside weight limit

- Runny eyes, odd colored or wall eyes (cataracts)
- Putty nose
- Bunches of white hairs or white toenails in colored rabbits
- Poor Condition

3) Packing for a Show

The key to success in rabbit shows is to be prepared. This involves making sure your rabbit meets the breed standard and arranging the rabbit properly for judging. There are further details available from a range of websites at the back of the book which should prove helpful.

However, you should also prepare yourself by bringing along an emergency kit, just in case.

Included in your emergency kit should be:

- Nail clippers – for emergency nail trimming

- Antibiotic ointment

- Band-Aids – for minor injuries to self, not rabbit

- Hydrogen peroxide – for cleaning injuries and spots on white coats

- Slicker brush – to smooth rough coats

- Black felt-tip pen

- Business cards

- Paper towels – because you never know

- Scrap carpet square – for last-minute grooming

- Collapsible stool – when chairs are not available

- Extra clothes

- Supplies for your rabbits

Chapter Nine: Mini Lop Rabbits Care Sheet

1) *Mini Lop Facts Overview*

In this chapter you will find comprehensive summaries of many Mini Lop facts. Included in these synopses is valuable information about the breed itself as well as cage requirements, nutritional needs and breeding information. You will also learn some valuable tips for handling your rabbit, dealing with shedding and introducing your rabbit to your children.

a) Basic Information

Scientific Name: Oryctolagus cuniculus

Classification: small breed

Alternative Names: dwarf lop (UK)

Weight: the maximum weight defined by the ARBA weight limits and showroom classes is 6.5 lbs. (2.72 kg) in U.S. and as defined by the BRC in the UK is 5 lbs. 4 oz. (2.38 kg)

Body Shape: medium-sized, thick set and round

Body Structure: heavily muscled, well balanced

Coat: medium-length, thick and dense

Coat Color: black, blue, blue-eyed white, chestnut agouti, chinchilla, chocolate, orange, opal, lynx, lilac, tri color, ruby-eyed white and white

Ears: lopped (pendulous rather than erect)

Diet: herbivorous

Foods: Timothy hay, commercial rabbit pellets, vegetables and fruits

Supplements: generally not required if the diet is sufficient in fiber and protein

Lifespan: average 7 to 10 years

b) Cage Set-up Guide

Location Options: indoor vs. outdoor

Cage Types: single-level, multi-level, open pen

Cage Materials: metal cage with wire mesh sides, solid bottom

Bedding: non-toxic pellets, fresh hay, newspaper

Accessories: water bottle, food bowls, hay compartment, litter pan, chew toys and shelter

c) Feeding Guide

Diet Basics: low protein, high fiber

Main Diet: Timothy hay and grass

Nutritional Breakdown: 16% or less protein, at least 15% to 20% fiber

Ingredients to Avoid: corn, binders, feed dust

Supplemental Foods: High quality alfalfa pellets, fresh fruits, fresh vegetables

Amount to Feed: 0.75 to 1 oz. (21.3 to 28.3g) pellets per pound bodyweight, unlimited hay, and small portion of fruit/vegetable daily

Other Needs: unlimited supply of fresh de-chlorinated water

d) **Breeding Tips**

Sexually Mature (Doe): 5 to 6 months average

Sexually Mature (Buck): 7 to 8 months average

Breeding Age: after 6 months

Litter Size: 1 to 2 (first breeding); 2 to 4 average

Gestation Period: lasts about 31 days

Birthing Process: 20 minutes average

Eyes and Ears Open: about 10 days

Solid Food: begin sampling around 3 weeks

Weaning: around 5 to 6 weeks

2) Handling a Mini Lop Rabbit

It is important to remember that Mini Lop Rabbits are fragile creatures so you need to use caution when handling them. The first thing you need to know is that you must never pick up your rabbit by the ears. When you first bring your rabbit home you should give it a day or two to get used to the new environment before you try to hold it.

When you feel your rabbit is ready, offer it a few treats to encourage the rabbit to approach you on its own. Once your rabbit approaches you, begin petting it gently on the back and ears. If your rabbit responds well to this treatment you can try picking it up. Make sure to support your rabbit's feet and hold the rabbit's body against your chest. Do not let very young children handle the rabbit and be careful when putting it back down.

3) Mini Lop Rabbit Shedding

Some rabbits shed more than others but most breeds shed every three months. Like cats, rabbits are very clean animals and they like to groom themselves. Unlike cats, however, rabbits cannot vomit – thus, if they consume too much hair it could form a ball in the stomach and cause serious health problems and could cause Wool Block. For this reason, it is essential that you brush your rabbit at least once a week to remove loose and dead hairs from its coat. During shedding seasons, you may need to brush Mini Lop Rabbits once a day or even multiple times a day to keep up.

4) Introducing Rabbits to Children

Mini Lop Rabbits are a very gentle breed so they have the capacity to get along with children. If your children are not properly educated in how to handle the rabbit, however, it could result in accidental injury. Before you bring your rabbit home, make sure to talk to your children about the responsibilities of their new pet. Teach your children how to properly hold the rabbit and warn them that the rabbit might be frightened by loud noises.

Once you bring your rabbit home, give it time to acclimatize to its new surroundings. After your rabbit has become comfortable at home you can try introducing it to your children. Hold the rabbit securely in your arms and let your child pet it gently. If your rabbit is calm, you can try setting it down on the ground so your child can pet it. Do not let your children pick the rabbit up unless they are old enough to know how to do so properly.

Chapter Ten: Frequently Asked Questions

Q: *Should I buy one Mini Lop Rabbit or two?*

A: The answer to this question has many variables. If you are a new rabbit owner, you may find it easier to care for one rabbit than to care for two. If you really think about it, however, caring for two rabbits is not a significant amount more work than caring for one – you can keep them both in the same cage and offer them the same food. You should also consider the fact that Mini Lop Rabbits are friendly, social creatures and they enjoy the company of other rabbits. It is best to keep these rabbits in pairs or groups of three but they can be kept alone if provided with enough care and attention. If you are going to keep them outside, always keep at least two rabbits together.

Q: *What kinds of costs should I be prepared for?*

A: Mini Lop Rabbit owners are responsible for a number of costs, some of which recur on a monthly basis. When you are just getting started you will need to cover the costs for the rabbit cage and accessories as well as the rabbit itself. After setting up the cage and buying the rabbit, you will then need to purchase food and bedding on a monthly basis. You should also be prepared to cover additional costs such as veterinary care and replacement items.

Q: *Can Mini Lop Rabbits be kept outside?*

A: Pet rabbits can generally be kept outside in a hutch but you should think carefully before choosing this option.

Rabbits that are kept outside are more likely to be exposed to disease and there is also the risk of predators getting into the cage and harming or killing your rabbits. Keeping your rabbits outdoors may also mean that you do not pay as much attention to them as you would if they were indoors – for this reason, it is essential that outdoor rabbits be kept in pairs or trios.

Q: *What precautions should I take when buying from a breeder?*

A: You should take the same precautions in buying from a breeder as you would in a pet store or shelter. You will need to examine the individual rabbits to make sure they are healthy before you even begin to talk about purchasing one. In addition to checking the health of the stock, you should also determine the breeder's experience and credentials. Ask the breeder questions to determine how much they know about the breed, how much experience they have and whether or not they have the required license or registration to breed rabbits legally.

Q: *Is it okay to buy Mini Lop Rabbits from online ads?*

A: Purchasing any animals from an online ad is risky for a number of reasons. First, you will not be able to view the animal before purchase to make sure that it is in good condition. Second, buying online probably means that the animal will have to be shipped. The shipping process can be extremely stressful and dangerous for animals because they may be exposed to extreme temperatures and rough handling. Please avoid buying animals online.

Q: *What are the benefits of adopting an adult rabbit?*

A: Many people prefer to buy baby rabbits because they want to raise the rabbit themselves. While this is a wonderful experience, there are also several unique benefits involved in adopting an adult rabbit. Adult rabbits are more likely to already be litter trained which will save you the hassle of having to do it yourself. It is also more likely that the rabbit will already be spayed or neutered because this is a policy most shelters enforce. Adopting an adult rabbit may also be a little cheaper than buying a baby rabbit from a pet store or breeder but more importantly you will be giving a home to an animal that needs it. It is definitely worth investigating.

Q: *Do I need to give my rabbit supplements?*

A: As long as you provide your Mini Lop Rabbits with a healthy, varied diet you should not need to give them any supplements Giving your rabbits some supplements can help to boost their nutrition. One option is to provide your rabbit with a salt or mineral block. In addition to giving your rabbits iodine and other minerals, it can also help relieve their boredom. Small (teaspoon size) pieces of fruit such as banana, apple or oatmeal and herbs can be used as treats but should only be given occasionally. Do not give your rabbits any human food or vitamin supplements without checking with your veterinarian first.

Q: *Should I refill my rabbit's bowl of pellets during the day?*

A: No. If you keep refilling your rabbit's bowl, your rabbit may eat more of the pellets than hay and get bloated. Hay and vegetables are the most important parts of your rabbit's daily diet so you should do what you can to encourage him to eat those foods. Commercial pellets are a supplement to your rabbit's diet of hay and vegetables.

Q: *Can I build my own rabbit cage?*

A: Yes, you can build your own rabbit cage as long as you use the appropriate materials and make it the right size. The easiest way to make your own rabbit cage is to use stackable wire cubes to create a multi-level cage. Insert wooden dowels through the gaps to create supports for wooden shelves and line the shelves with towels to make them more comfortable for your rabbit.

Q: *Can I let my rabbit play outside?*

A: Yes, you can let your rabbit play outside as long as you take a few precautions. First, it is important that your rabbit receives all the necessary vaccinations to keep him protected against disease. Second, you should build or buy an outdoor rabbit run that will keep your rabbit safe while he is outside. Even while your rabbit is confined to the run you should keep an eye on him.

Q: *How big should my rabbit cage be?*

A: In response to this question, many experienced rabbit owners will reply "the bigger the better." At minimum, however, your rabbit cage should be wide enough for your rabbit to stretch all the way out. The cage should be about four times your rabbit's size in length so that it can make three or four hops from one end to the other. It should also be tall enough for it to stand on its hind legs. Keeping your rabbit in a cage too small can result in health problems.

Q: *How often should I clean my rabbit's cage?*

A: The best answer to this question is "as often as necessary". If you have multiple rabbits in one cage or one messy rabbit, you may need to clean out the cage more often than you would for a single rabbit. Generally, you should plan to change your rabbit's bedding once a week but you may need to clean the litter box two or three times within that same period of time.

Q: *What vaccinations are required for rabbit?*

A: Vaccinations are not required but certain ones are highly recommended. The two most important vaccines for rabbits are against myxomatosis and rabbit hemorrhagic disease (RHD) or known in the UK as viral haemorrhagic disease (VHD). Both of these diseases are very serious and often fatal. Aside from preventive vaccination, treatments for these diseases are typically ineffective.

Q: *Do I need to have my rabbit examined by a vet?*

A: Again, it is your choice whether or not you provide your rabbit with routine veterinary care. Some rabbit owners prefer to save themselves the expense of veterinary visits while others see the value in it. The benefit of taking your rabbit in for regular check-ups is that you can catch diseases and conditions in the early stages and provide treatment. You can also keep your rabbit up to date on recommended vaccinations.

Q: *What are the health benefits of spaying/neutering?*

A: Some rabbits exhibit behavioral changes if they are not spayed or neutered -- they may become more aggressive and they may spray urine. For female rabbits, spaying greatly reduces the risk for uterine cancer. Uterine cancer is one of the most common causes of death in un-spayed rabbits and it is often untreatable by the time a diagnosis is made. Neutering male rabbits will help prevent them from fighting with other rabbits which could also serve to extend their lives.

Q: *At what age can I begin breeding my Mini Lop Rabbits?*

A: Female Mini Lop Rabbits are generally considered sexually mature at 5 to 6 months while males are considered sexually mature at 7 to 8 months.

Q: *Can't I just keep a male and female in the same cage together if I want to breed them?*

A: Keeping male and female rabbits together in the same cage will result in breeding, but it may not be a healthy situation for your rabbits. After a female rabbit becomes pregnant, she will enter a 31-day gestation period. During that time it is not possible for the female to become pregnant again but the male may continue to attempt to breed. This can be exhausting for the female rabbit and dangerous if the male becomes aggressive in his advances. It is best to separate the sexes after breeding to ensure that the female rabbit is able to rest and the babies develop properly.

Q: *Should I worry if the Dam doesn't begin feeding the babies right away?*

A: No. It is not uncommon for Mini Lop Rabbit Dams to wait a day or two before they begin feeding their young. If she has not begun feeding them after two days, however, you may want to consider using a foster mother. If you introduce the litter to a foster mother while they are young enough, she will be less likely to reject them.

Q: *Can I move the babies from the nest box to clean it?*

A: No. If you observe the female rabbit you will notice that she never moves the babies from the nest box. When Mini Lop Rabbits are born they are virtually hairless so they depend on the nest box and their collective body heat to survive. If you move the baby rabbits from the nest box, they could die from exposure.

Q: *Will I need a license if I plan to breed my Mini Lop Rabbits?*

A: The answer to this question varies depending where you live. In most cases, a license is not required for individuals to keep Mini Lop Rabbits as pets. If you live in the United States and plan to breed your rabbits, however, you may need to obtain a license. A license is not required in the U.K. to breed rabbits. Be sure to check with your local council to find the answer to this question.

Chapter Eleven: Common Myths Debunked

1) You Should Never Feed Your Rabbit Grass

– FALSE

There is a common myth that feeding your rabbit grass will cause bloat and/or diarrhea. In reality, grass can actually be good for your rabbit! After all, wild rabbits eat a diet that consists primarily of grass, right? You do, however, need to be careful about letting your rabbit munch on the grass in your yard. If you use fertilizers, pesticides or other chemical lawn treatments it could be dangerous for your rabbit. As an alternative, try growing a pot or container of grass for your rabbit indoors without using fertilizers, pesticides or other chemical lawn treatments.

2) You Should Never Feed Your Rabbit Fruit

– FALSE

This myth is founded on the idea that feeding rabbit fruit or other sweet foods encourages the growth of bacteria. While refined sugars are most certainly not ideal for rabbits to eat, natural sugars (fructose) like those found in fruit are perfectly okay. Fruit should be limited to 1 small piece per day with the majority of the rabbit's food being vegetable-based. In fact, grass and hay naturally contain some of this sugar anyway.

3) Rabbits Need to be Kept in Pairs

– FALSE

If you perform some basic research on keeping rabbits as pets you are likely to find a number of resources claiming that rabbits need to be kept in pairs or they might become "lonely". Keep in mind that "lonely" is a human emotion – rabbits do not have human feelings. As long as you provide your rabbit with plenty of attention and human interaction, it will be perfectly fine on its own. However, it is essential that outdoor rabbits be kept in pairs or trios.

4) Rabbits Don't Need to go to the Vet

– FALSE

While rabbits may not require a routine vaccination schedule like dogs and cats, it is recommended that you seek advice from your vet regarding the recommended vaccines. These will depend on where you live. Vaccinations are also often required for getting pet insurance, holiday boarding and attending events. After reading the health section of this book you should know that many rabbit diseases progress rapidly, often without showing any symptoms. This being the case, taking your rabbit to the vet once or twice a year may be the only way to catch diseases before they progress beyond repair.

5) Pet Rabbits are Best Kept Outdoors

– FALSE

There are benefits to keeping a rabbit outdoors but you should think carefully before you do so. Some rabbit owners claim that rabbits should ONLY be kept outdoors while others claim that indoors is best. The choice is ultimately yours to make but keep in mind that outdoor rabbits are more likely to be exposed to disease, inclement weather and extreme temperatures. They may also not get as much attention as indoor rabbits which could affect their temperament and overall well-being.

6) Rabbits Love to be Picked Up

– FALSE

While many rabbit breeds including the Mini Lop are very friendly by nature, they generally do not like being picked up and held. You must appreciate that being held so high off the ground can be a frightening experience for a rabbit, so it is best to enjoy their company by getting down on the floor and joining them at their level.

Chapter Twelve: Relevant Websites

Shopping

When you start looking around the internet it can take some time to track down exactly what you are looking for.

A one-stop shop for all your rabbit needs is what is required and the sites below offer you the convenience of pulling together many of the best products from around the web. Enjoy Shopping!

United States Website
www.rabbitsorbunnies.com

United Kingdom Website
www.rabbitsorbunnies.co.uk

In this chapter you will find a number of helpful websites full of information on the Mini Lop Rabbit breed. In these websites you will find information for both residents of the U.S.A. and the U.K. under the following categories:

- Food for Mini Lop Rabbits

- Care for Mini Lop Rabbits

- Health Information for Mini Lop Rabbits

- General Information for Mini Lop Rabbits

- Showing Mini Lop Rabbits

1) Food for Mini Lop Rabbits

These websites will provide you with information about feeding your Mini Lop Rabbits a healthy diet. You will receive information about your rabbit's nutritional needs, food options and more.

United States Websites:

"Feeding Your Mini Lop the Correct Foods." Lisa's Mini Lop Bunnies. http://lisasminilops.weebly.com/fresh-foods-good-and-toxic.html

"Feeding Your Rabbit the Correct Way." RabbitMatters.com. www.rabbitmatters.com/feeding-your-rabbit.html

Logsdon, Alexandra. "Feeding Your Pet Bunny for a Long Healthy Life." Zooh Corner. www.mybunny.org/info/rabbit_nutrition.htm

United Kingdom Websites:

"Bunny Care." Dee Mill Rabbits. www.miniloprabbit.co.uk/5.html

"General Rabbit Care." JJ's Lops.co.uk. www.jjs-lops.co.uk/rabbit-care.html

"Rabbit – Facts and Care Sheet." Freshfields Animal Rescue.
www.freshfieldsrescue.org.uk/images/uploads/articles/Rabbit_care_sheet1.pdf

"Feeding Your Rabbit." Croft Veterinary Surgeons.
www.croftvets.co.uk/rabbits/feeding-your-rabbit

2) Care for Mini Lop Rabbits

The websites in this section will provide you with information about caring for Mini Lop Rabbits. You will find information regarding housing and raising rabbits as well as tips for purchasing a rabbit from a breeder.

United States Websites:

"Rabbit Care and Breeding Info." Hoppin' Herd of Hares.
www.hoppinherdofhares.com/rabbitcare.html

"Housing of Rabbits." The Merck Veterinary Manual.
www.merckmanuals.com/vet/exotic_and_laboratory_animals/rabbits/housing_of_rabbits.html

"Rabbit Care." SGT Hoppers Rabbitry.
http://sgthoppersrabbitry.com/Rabbit_Care.html

United Kingdom Websites:

"Rabbits." The Royal Society for the Prevention of Cruelty to Animals.
www.rspca.org.uk/allaboutanimals/pets/rabbits

"Care of Your Rabbit." Christine Hunter's Lops.
www.dwarflops.co.uk/Rabbit_Care.htm

"Thinking of Buying a Rabbit?" Scottish Dwarf Lops.
www.scottishdwarflops.co.uk/thinking.html

3) Health Information for Mini Lop Rabbits

The websites in this section will provide you with information about keeping your Mini Lop Rabbits healthy. You will find information about common health problems, vaccinations and other health-related information.

United States Websites:

"A Few Common Illnesses in Bunnies." Lisa's Mini Lop Bunnies.
http://lisasminilops.weebly.com/mini-lop-illness.html

"Rabbit Health – With Proper Care Rabbits Make Charming Companions." RabbitMatters.com.
www.rabbitmatters.com/rabbitcare.html

"Parasitic Diseases of Rabbits." The Merck Veterinary Manual.
www.merckmanuals.com/vet/exotic_and_laboratory_anim
als/rabbits/parasitic_diseases_of_rabbits.html

United Kingdom Websites:

"Health." The People's Dispensary for Sick Animals.
www.pdsa.org.uk/pet-health-advice/rabbits/health

"Bunny Care." Dee Mill Rabbits.
www.miniloprabbit.co.uk/5.html

"Health." Ayrshire Dwarf and Mini Lops.
www.ayrshiredwarflops.co.uk/care-info/health.aspx

4) General Information for Mini Lop Rabbits

The following websites will provide you with general information about Mini Lop Rabbits – here you will find information regarding the history of the Mini Lop breed, general facts and owner testimonials.

United States Websites:

"Mini Lop Rabbits." Animal-World.
http://animal-
world.com/encyclo/critters/rabbits/minilop.php

"Mini Lop Rabbit." RabbitMatters.com.
www.rabbitmatters.com/mini-lop.html

"Mini Lop History." Lisa's Mini Lop Bunnies.
http://lisasminilops.weebly.com/mini-lop-history.html

"Miniature Lop Rabbits." Elti Bunnies.
http://elti.webs.com/bunnyinfoquestions.htm

United Kingdom Websites:

"Dwarf Lop, the proper guide"
www.rabbitmatters.com/dwarf-lop.html

"Dwarf Lop(UK)"
www.bunnyhugga.com/a-to-z/breeds/dwarf-lop-uk.html

 "Choosing Your Perfect Pet Rabbit." Rabbit Welfare
Association and Fund.
www.rabbitwelfare.co.uk/resources/?section=breeds.html

"Rabbit – Dwarf Lop Breed Profile." PetPlanet.co.uk.
www.petplanet.co.uk/small_breed_profile.asp?sbid=6

5) Showing Mini Lop Rabbits

The following websites will provide you with information
that will help you should you wish to know more about
showing Mini Lop Rabbits in either the U.S.A. or the U.K.

You will find information regarding the breed standard, how points are awarded and how to prepare for shows.

United States Websites:

"Posing and Evaluating Mini Lops." Hoppin' Herd of Hares. www.hoppinherdofhares.com/posing.html

"The Mini Lop Rabbit Standard." The Ohio Mini Lop Rabbit Club. www.ohiominilop.com/

"Mini Lop Standard." Texas Mini Lop Rabbit Club. http://texasmlrc.tripod.com/standard.htm

United Kingdom Websites:

"Dwarf Lop Standard." National French and Dwarf Lop Club. www.nfdlc.com/standard.html

"Dwarf Lop." The British Rabbit Council. www.thebrc.org/standards/L3-Lop%20Dwarf.pdf

"Dwarf Lop Standard." Welsh Lop Circle. www.welshlopcircle.co.uk/#/dwarf-lop-standard/4540373395

Index

Index

Index

G

H

I

K

L

Index

Index

Index

Photo Credits

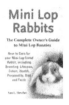

Cover Design:- Liliana Gonzalez Garcia, ipublicidades.com (info@ipublicidades.com)

Title Page Photo by Miniaturelop
http://commons.wikimedia.org/wiki/File:Miniature_Lop3_-_Grey.jpg

Photo by SequereMe
http://commons.wikimedia.org/wiki/File%3ADeutscher_Klein-Widder.JPG

Photo by Flickr user Carly & Art
www.flickr.com/photos/wiredwitch/2885894183

Photo by Flickr user _-Cat-
www.flickr.com/photos/37776029@N08/5184211012

Photo by Flickr user Jpockele
www.flickr.com/photos/jpockele/298971090

Photo by Loki db4
http://commons.wikimedia.org/wiki/File:Daisy_Mini_lop.jpg

Photo by Flickr user Justin Snow

www.flickr.com/photos/justinandelise/4398870686

Photo by Miniaturelop

http://commons.wikimedia.org/wiki/File:Miniature_Lop_-_Side_View.jpg

Photo by Miniaturelop

http://commons.wikimedia.org/wiki/File:Miniature_Lop.jpg

Photo by Flickr user Jpockele,

www.flickr.com/photos/jpockele/239246622

Photo by MRM82 via Wikimedia Commons,
http://commons.wikimedia.org/wiki/File:S7000021.JPG

Photo by Flickr user Valeehill,
www.flickr.com/photos/valeehill/5449080898

Photo by Miniaturelop
http://commons.wikimedia.org/wiki/File:Miniature_Lop2_-_Grey.jpg

Photo by Lucki19
http://commons.wikimedia.org/wiki/File:Mini_Lop.jpg

Photo by Franie Frou Frou
http://commons.wikimedia.org/wiki/File:Mini_lop.jpg

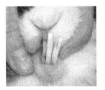

Photo by Uwe Gille
http://commons.wikimedia.org/wiki/File:Bradygnathia-superior-rabbit.jpg

Photo by Flickr user Spigoo
http://www.flickr.com/photos/spigoo/2099086

Photo by DeviantArt user Rabbitbreeder,
http://rabbitbreeder.deviantart.com/art/Newborn-Mini-Lops-347756893

Photo by Flickr Focus Photography NZ
www.flickr.com/photos/dancer4life17/5183725539

Photo by Miniaturelop
http://commons.wikimedia.org/wiki/File:Miniature_Lop_-_Grey.jpg

Photo by Flickr user David Masters,
www.flickr.com/photos/davidmasters/3697771255

Photo by Flickr user Justin Snow,
www.flickr.com/photos/justinandelise/4209781604

Photo by Amanda Warren (originally posted to Flickr as So shy)
http://commons.wikimedia.org/wiki/File:So_shy_Mini_Lop.jpg

Photo Credits

Photo by Flickr user Jlhopgood,
http://www.flickr.com/photos/jlhopgood/7609425742

Photo Courtesy www.rabbitsandbunnies.com

Photo by Luisa Blor
http://commons.wikimedia.org/wiki/File:Teddy_das_kaninnchen
.JPG

These works are licensed under the Creative Commons Attribution 2.0 Generic license and 3.0 Unported License. To view a copy of this license, visit http://creativecommons.org/licenses/by/3.0/ or send a letter to Creative Commons, 444 Castro Street, Suite 900, Mountain View, California, 94041, USA. [cc] BY

References

American Mini Lop Rabbit Club Website.
www.amlrc.com/

BRC Standards for Dwarf Lop
http://www.thebrc.org/standards/L3-Lop%20Dwarf.pdf

"Bunny Care." Dee Mill Rabbits.
www.miniloprabbit.co.uk/5.html

"Can I have a pet rabbit?" Department of Agriculture, Fisheries
and Forestry Biosecurity Queensland
http://www.daff.qld.gov.au/__data/assets/pdf_file/0009/57780/IP
A-Keeping-Rabbits-As-Pets-PA15.pdf

"Characteristics of a Mini Lop." Schmidt's Mini Lop Rabbits.
www.freewebs.com/schmidtminilops/theminilopstandard.htm

"Dwarf Lop Standard." National French and Dwarf Lop Club.
www.nfdlc.com/standard.html

"Fact Sheet – Dwarf Lop and Mini Lop Rabbit." Burke's
Backyard.
www.burkesbackyard.com.au/factsheets/Others/Dwarf-Lop-and-
Mini-Lop-Rabbit/1016

References

"Feeding Your Rabbit." Croft Veterinary Surgeons.
www.croftvets.co.uk/rabbits/feeding-your-rabbit

"Feeding Your Mini Lop the Correct Foods." Lisa's Mini Lop
Bunnies.
http://lisasminilops.weebly.com/fresh-foods-good-and-toxic.html

"Feeding Your Rabbit the Correct Way."
www.rabbitmatters.com/feeding-your-rabbit.html

"Litter Training"
http://rabbit.org/faq-litter-training-2/

Logsdon, Alexandra. "Feeding Your Pet Bunny for a Long
Healthy Life." Zooh Corner.
www.mybunny.org/info/rabbit_nutrition.htm

"Lop Color Guide." Hoppin' Herd of Hares.
www.hoppinherdofhares.com/lopcolorguide.html

"Mini Lop Colour Guide." Mini-Lops.
www.freewebs.com/mini-lops/minilopcolours.htm

"Mini Lop Rabbits." Animal-World.
http://animal-world.com/encyclo/critters/rabbits/minilop.php

"Points and Body Type." Ohio Mini Lop Rabbit Club.
www.ohiominilop.com/

"Posing and Evaluating Mini Lops." Hoppin' Herd of Hares.
www.hoppinherdofhares.com/posing.html

References

Rabbit Breeders.us
http://rabbitbreeders.us/mini-lop-rabbits

"Rabbit – Facts and Care Sheet." Freshfields Animal Rescue.
www.freshfieldsrescue.org.uk/images/uploads/articles/Rabbit_ca
re_sheet1.pdf

"The Mini Lop Rabbit Standard." The Ohio Mini Lop Rabbit
Club.
www.ohiominilop.com/

Wikipedia
http://en.wikipedia.org/wiki/Mini_Lop

Notes: